Elevating Your HTML Skill

BEYOND HTML FUNDAMENTAL

A comprehensive Guide to Advanced topics

Robert J. Smith

BASIC HTML TUTORIALS

BEYOND HTML FUNDAMENTAL

A COMPREHENCIVE GUIDE TO ADVANCED TOPICS

BY

ROBERT J. SMITH

TABLE OF CONTENTS

WHAT IS HTML?

HTML stands for HyperText Markup Language. It's the standard markup language used to create and structure content on the web. HTML provides a set of elements (tags) that define the structure and presentation of a webpage's content, such as text, images, links, forms, and more. These elements are represented using opening and closing tags, enclosed in angle brackets, and can include attributes to provide additional information about the element.

In essence, HTML is the backbone of web pages, allowing developers to create the structure and layout of a webpage's content, which is then interpreted by web browsers to display the content to users. Alongside other technologies like CSS (Cascading Style Sheets) and JavaScript, HTML forms the foundation of modern web development.

IMPORTANCE OF HTML IN WEB DEVELOPMENT

HTML plays a crucial role in web development for several reasons:

i. **Structure:** HTML defines the basic structure of a webpage, such as headings, paragraphs, lists, and more. It creates a hierarchical layout that organizes content and helps browsers understand how to display it.

ii. **Content:** HTML allows you to include various types of content on a webpage, such as text, images, videos, audio, and more. It's the medium through which information is presented to users.

iii. **Accessibility:** Properly structured HTML contributes to web accessibility, making it possible for users with disabilities to navigate and understand content using assistive technologies.

iv. **SEO (Search Engine Optimization):** Search engines use the HTML structure to understand the content and context of a webpage. Well-structured HTML can improve a website's search engine rankings and visibility.

v. **Semantics:** HTML5 introduced semantic elements like `<header>`, `<nav>`, `<article>`, and `<footer>`. These elements provide meaning to the structure, making it easier for developers and search engines to understand the purpose of different parts of a webpage.

vi. **Responsive Design:** HTML is essential for creating responsive web design, where websites adapt to different screen sizes and devices. Using HTML along with CSS and sometimes JavaScript, developers can create flexible layouts that look good on various devices.

vii.   **Forms:** HTML forms enable interaction with users, allowing them to submit data to a server for processing. This is crucial for various web applications, from simple contact forms to complex user registration systems.

viii.   **Links and Navigation:** HTML provides the foundation for creating hyperlinks, enabling users to navigate between different pages and resources on the internet.

ix.   **Consistency:** HTML ensures a consistent structure across different web browsers. While browser rendering engines may vary, adherence to HTML standards ensures a certain level of uniformity in how web content is displayed.

x.   **Interactivity:** Although HTML itself is not primarily responsible for interactivity, it often works in conjunction with JavaScript to create dynamic and interactive web applications.

HTML serves as the fundamental building block of web development, defining the structure, content, and organization of web pages. It's an essential language for creating user-friendly, accessible, and visually appealing websites.

CHOOSING A TEXT EDITOR

Choosing the right text editor is an important decision when getting started with HTML and web development. Here are a few popular options to consider:

i. **Visual Studio Code:** This is a highly popular and feature-rich code editor developed by Microsoft. It offers a wide range of extensions that can enhance your HTML development experience with features like syntax highlighting, auto-completion, and integrated version control.

ii. **Sublime Text:** Known for its speed and simplicity, Sublime Text is a lightweight text editor that's favored by many developers. It supports multiple programming languages, including HTML, and offers a clean and customizable interface.

iii. **Atom:** Atom is an open-source text editor developed by GitHub. It's highly customizable and has a strong community contributing to its extensive library of packages and themes. Atom is suitable for both beginners and experienced developers.

iv. **Brackets:** Adobe's Brackets is designed with web development in mind. It includes features like live preview and inline editing of CSS and JavaScript. It's particularly well-suited for front-end developers working on HTML and CSS.

v. **Notepad++:** If you're on Windows, Notepad++ is a lightweight and free text editor that supports various programming languages, including HTML. While it may not be as feature-rich as some other editors, it's simple and easy to use.

vi. **TextMate:** Primarily for macOS, TextMate offers a balance between simplicity and functionality. It supports syntax highlighting, macros, and offers a variety of bundles for different programming languages.

When choosing a text editor, consider factors like your comfort with the interface, the availability of extensions or plugins, the specific features you need (like live preview, version control integration, etc.), and whether it aligns with your operating system.

Ultimately, the best text editor for you will depend on your personal preferences and workflow. It's a good idea to try out a few different options and see which one feels the most comfortable and suits your needs as you learn HTML and web development.

BASIC HTML TEMPLATE

Creating your first HTML file is a simple and exciting step in your web development journey. Here's how to do it:

i. Choose a Text Editor: Open your preferred text editor. As mentioned earlier, popular choices include Visual Studio Code, Sublime Text, Atom, and others.

ii. Create a New File: Click on "File" and then select "New" to create a new file. Alternatively, you can use keyboard shortcuts like Ctrl+N (Windows) or Command+N (Mac).

iii. Write HTML Code: In the new file, start by typing the basic structure of an HTML document. Here's a template to begin with:

```html
<!DOCTYPE html>
<html>
<head>
  <title>Your Page Title</title>
</head>
<body>
  <h1>Hello, World!</h1>
  <p>This is my first HTML file.</p>
</body>
</html>
```

This example includes the essential components of an HTML document: `<!DOCTYPE html>`, the opening `<html>` tag, `<head>` for metadata, and `<body>` for content. Replace "Your Page Title" with the title you want for your webpage.

iv.   Save the File: Save the file with an ".html" extension. Choose a meaningful name for your file, like "index.html" for your homepage. Make sure to select the appropriate file type ("All Files" or "HTML Files") when saving.

v.   View in a Browser: Once the file is saved, open your web browser and use the "File" > "Open File" option to open the HTML file you just created. Alternatively, you can simply drag and drop the file into the browser.

You should see the content you've written within the browser. Congratulations, you've created your first HTML file!

As you learn more about HTML, you can explore additional elements, attributes, and styles to enhance your webpage's appearance and functionality.

Here's a basic HTML template that you can use as a starting point for your web pages:

```html
<!DOCTYPE html>

<html>

<head>

  <meta charset="UTF-8">

  <meta name="viewport" content="width=device-width, initial-scale=1.0">

  <title>Your Page Title</title>

  <link rel="stylesheet" href="styles.css"> <!-- Link to your CSS file -->

</head>

<body>

  <header>

    <h1>Your Website Name</h1>
```

```html
<nav>
  <ul>
    <li><a href="#">Home</a></li>
    <li><a href="#">About</a></li>
    <li><a href="#">Services</a></li>
    <li><a href="#">Contact</a></li>
  </ul>
</nav>
</header>

<main>
  <section>
    <h2>About Us</h2>
    <p>Welcome to our website! We are dedicated to...</p>
  </section>
```

```html
<section>

    <h2>Our Services</h2>

    <ul>

        <li>Service 1</li>

        <li>Service 2</li>

        <li>Service 3</li>

    </ul>

</section>

</main>


<footer>

    <p>&copy; 2023 Your Website. All rights reserved.</p>

</footer>

</body>

</html>
```

This template includes the essential structure of an HTML document, as well as some basic elements commonly found in web pages:

- `<meta>` tags for character encoding and viewport settings.

- `<title>` for setting the title of the webpage (displayed in the browser's tab).

- A link to an external stylesheet (`styles.css`) for applying CSS styles.

- A header with a navigation menu.

- A main content area with two sections.

- A footer with copyright information.

Feel free to customize the content and structure according to your needs. As you learn more about HTML and web development, you can expand upon this template and add more advanced features and styles.

HEAD AND BODY SECTIONS

The HTML document is divided into two main sections: the `<head>` section and the `<body>` section. Here's what each section does:

1. `<head>` Section:

The `<head>` section contains metadata and information about the document. It doesn't display visible content on the webpage, but it provides essential information for browsers and search engines. Common elements within the `<head>` section include:

- `<title>`: Sets the title of the webpage, which appears in the browser's tab or window title bar.

- `<meta>`: Contains metadata about the document, such as character encoding and viewport settings.

- `<link>`: Links to external resources like stylesheets (CSS) or icons.

- `<script>`: Links to or embeds JavaScript code that affects the behavior of the webpage.

Here's an example of a `<head>` section:

```html
<head>
    <meta charset="UTF-8">
    <meta name="viewport" content="width=device-width, initial-scale=1.0">
    <title>Your Page Title</title>
    <link rel="stylesheet" href="styles.css">
</head>
```

2. `<body>` Section:

The `<body>` section contains the visible content of the webpage that users see and interact with. This is where you place headings, paragraphs, images, links, forms, and other elements. The content you include within the `<body>` section will be rendered and displayed on the webpage.

Here's an example of a `<body>` section:

```html
<body>
  <header>
    <h1>Your Website Name</h1>
    <nav>
      <ul>
        <li><a href="#">Home</a></li>
        <li><a href="#">About</a></li>
        <li><a href="#">Services</a></li>
        <li><a href="#">Contact</a></li>
      </ul>
    </nav>
  </header>
  <main>
  <section>
    <h2>About Us</h2>
    <p>Welcome to our website! We are dedicated to...</p>
  </section>
```

```html
    <section>
        <h2>Our Services</h2>
        <ul>
            <li>Service 1</li>
            <li>Service 2</li>
            <li>Service 3</li>
        </ul>
    </section>
  </main>


  <footer>
    <p>&copy; 2023 Your Website. All rights reserved.</p>
  </footer>
 </body>
```

Remember, the content within the `<head>` section provides information about the document, while the content within the `<body>` section is what users actually see and interact with on the webpage.

HEADINGS

Headings in HTML are used to define the structure and hierarchy of your content. HTML provides six levels of headings, from `<h1>` (highest importance) to `<h6>` (lowest importance). Here's how you can use headings in HTML:

```html
<!DOCTYPE html>

<html>

<head>

  <title>Headings Example</title>

</head>

<body>

  <h1>This is Heading 1</h1>

  <p>This is some content under Heading 1.</p>


  <h2>This is Heading 2</h2>
```

```
<p>This is some content under Heading 2.</p>

<h3>This is Heading 3</h3>

<p>This is some content under Heading 3.</p>

<h4>This is Heading 4</h4>

<p>This is some content under Heading 4.</p>

<h5>This is Heading 5</h5>

<p>This is some content under Heading 5.</p>

<h6>This is Heading 6</h6>

<p>This is some content under Heading 6.</p>

</body>

</html>

```

In this example, each heading level indicates a decreasing level of importance or subordination. Typically, `<h1>` is used for the main title of the page, while `<h2>` through `<h6>` are used to represent subsections or different levels of content within the page.

Search engines and assistive technologies for users with disabilities use heading tags to understand the structure and organization of your content. Using headings appropriately not only enhances the visual appearance of your page but also contributes to accessibility and search engine optimization.

PARAGRAPHS

Paragraphs in HTML are used to group and structure blocks of text content. You can create paragraphs using the `<p>` element. Here's how to use paragraphs in HTML:

```html

<!DOCTYPE html>

<html>
```

```html
<head>
  <title>Paragraphs Example</title>
</head>
<body>
  <h1>Welcome to My Website</h1>
  <p>This is the first paragraph of text. It provides some introductory information about the topic.</p>


  <p>This is another paragraph. It continues the discussion on the topic.</p>


  <h2>Benefits of Our Product</h2>
  <p>Our product offers several benefits:</p>
  <ul>
    <li>Increased efficiency</li>
    <li>Enhanced productivity</li>
    <li>Cost savings</li>
  </ul>
```

```html
<p>Feel free to <a href="#">contact us</a> to learn more
about our product offerings.</p>

</body>

</html>
```

In this example, the `<p>` element is used to define paragraphs
of text. You can include any amount of text within the `<p>`
tags. Each `<p>` element represents a separate paragraph.

Paragraphs are an essential element for organizing and
presenting textual content on your webpage. They help create
a clear and readable structure for your users, making it easier
to understand and engage with your content.

BOLD AND ITALICS

You can apply formatting to your text in HTML using the
`<strong>` and `<em>` elements to make text bold and italic,
respectively. Additionally, you can use the `<b>` and `<i>`
elements, but they are generally considered outdated for
semantic purposes. Here's how you can use these elements:

```html
<!DOCTYPE html>
<html>
<head>
  <title>Formatting Example</title>
</head>
<body>
  <p>This is <strong>bold text</strong>.</p>
  <p>This is <em>italic text</em>.</p>

  <p>This is <b>also bold text</b>.</p>
  <p>This is <i>also italic text</i>.</p>
</body>
</html>
```

In the example above, both the `<strong>` and `<b>` elements are used to make text bold, and both the `<em>` and `<i>` elements are used to make text italic. However, `<strong>` and `<em>` are considered more semantically meaningful because they convey importance and emphasis respectively, whereas `<b>` and `<i>` were traditionally used for presentational purposes.

It's a good practice to use `<strong>` for strong emphasis and `<em>` for italic emphasis, as they convey meaning and can assist search engines and assistive technologies in understanding the content better.

LINE BREAKS

In HTML, you can use the `<br>` element to create line breaks within your content. This is useful when you want to insert a new line without creating a new paragraph. Here's how you can use the `<br>` element:

```html
<!DOCTYPE html>
<html>
<head>
    <title>Line Breaks Example</title>
</head>
<body>
    <p>This is some text with a line break.<br>
    The content after the line break continues on a new line.</p>


    <p>You can also use multiple line breaks to create more space between lines:<br><br>
    Like this.</p>
</body>
</html>
```

In the example above, the `<br>` element is used to insert line breaks within paragraphs. You can place the `<br>` element wherever you want to introduce a new line within a block of text.

Keep in mind that while line breaks can be useful in specific situations, it's generally better to use proper HTML structure and CSS to control the layout and spacing of your content. Using line breaks excessively can result in less maintainable and more difficult-to-style code.

ORDERED LISTS

Ordered lists in HTML are used to present items in a sequentially numbered or lettered format. You can create ordered lists using the `<ol>` (ordered list) element and the `<li>` (list item) element to define each list item. Here's how you can use ordered lists:

```html
<!DOCTYPE html>

<html>

<head>

  <title>Ordered List Example</title>

</head>

<body>

  <h2>Steps to Bake a Cake</h2>

  <ol>

    <li>Preheat the oven to 350°F (175°C).</li>
```

```
      <li>Grease and flour the cake pans.</li>

      <li>In a mixing bowl, combine the dry ingredients.</li>

      <li>In another bowl, whisk together the wet
ingredients.</li>

      <li>Gradually add the wet mixture to the dry mixture and
mix well.</li>

      <li>Pour the batter into the prepared pans.</li>

      <li>Bake in the preheated oven for 25-30 minutes.</li>

      <li>Remove the cakes from the oven and let them
cool.</li>

      <li>Frost and decorate the cooled cakes.</li>

   </ol>

</body>

</html>

```
```

In the example above, the `<ol>` element is used to create an
ordered list, and each list item is defined using the `<li>`
```

element. The browser will automatically number or letter the list items based on the order in which they appear in the code.

Ordered lists are a great way to present information with a specific order or hierarchy, such as step-by-step instructions, rankings, or any other content that needs a sequential structure.

UNORDERED LISTS

Unordered lists in HTML are used to present items in a bulleted format without any particular sequence. You can create unordered lists using the `<ul>` (unordered list) element and the `<li>` (list item) element to define each list item. Here's how you can use unordered lists:

```html
<!DOCTYPE html>

<html>

<head>

    <title>Unordered List Example</title>

</head>
```

```html
<body>

  <h2>Fruits</h2>

  <ul>

    <li>Apples</li>

    <li>Oranges</li>

    <li>Bananas</li>

    <li>Strawberries</li>

  </ul>


  <h2>Colors</h2>

  <ul>

    <li>Red</li>

    <li>Blue</li>

    <li>Green</li>

    <li>Yellow</li>

  </ul>

</body>
```

```
</html>

```

In the example above, the `<ul>` element is used to create an unordered list, and each list item is defined using the `<li>` element. The browser will automatically display bullet points (or other symbols, depending on the browser) for each list item.

Unordered lists are great for presenting items that don't have a specific order or sequence. They are often used to showcase options, features, or any collection of items where the order doesn't matter.

NESTED LISTS

Nested lists in HTML allow you to create lists within lists, adding a hierarchical structure to your content. You can create both ordered and unordered nested lists. Here's how you can use nested lists:

```html

<!DOCTYPE html>

<html>
```

```html
<head>
    <title>Nested List Example</title>
</head>
<body>
    <h2>Grocery List</h2>
    <ul>
        <li>Fruits</li>
        <ul>
            <li>Apples</li>
            <li>Oranges</li>
            <li>Bananas</li>
        </ul>
        <li>Vegetables</li>
        <ul>
            <li>Carrots</li>
            <li>Broccoli</li>
            <li>Spinach</li>
```

```
</ul>

<li>Dairy</li>

<ul>

  <li>Milk</li>

  <li>Cheese</li>

  <li>Yogurt</li>

</ul>

</ul>


<h2>Steps to Make a Sandwich</h2>

<ol>

  <li>Choose your bread type</li>

  <li>Add your favorite spreads</li>

  <li>Add your desired fillings</li>

  <ol>

    <li>Lettuce</li>

    <li>Tomato</li>
```

```
        <li>Cheese</li>

        <li>Meat</li>

      </ol>

      <li>Put the sandwich together</li>

      <li>Enjoy!</li>

    </ol>

  </body>

</html>
```

In the example above, you can see both ordered and unordered nested lists. For nested lists, you simply include a new `<ul>` (unordered list) or `<ol>` (ordered list) within a list item `<li>` of an outer list.

Nested lists are useful when you want to show a hierarchy or subcategories within your content, such as sub-options within a main option or substeps within a main step.

CREATING HYPERLINKS

Creating hyperlinks in HTML allows you to link to other web pages, documents, or resources. You can use the `<a>` (anchor) element to create hyperlinks. Here's how you can create hyperlinks:

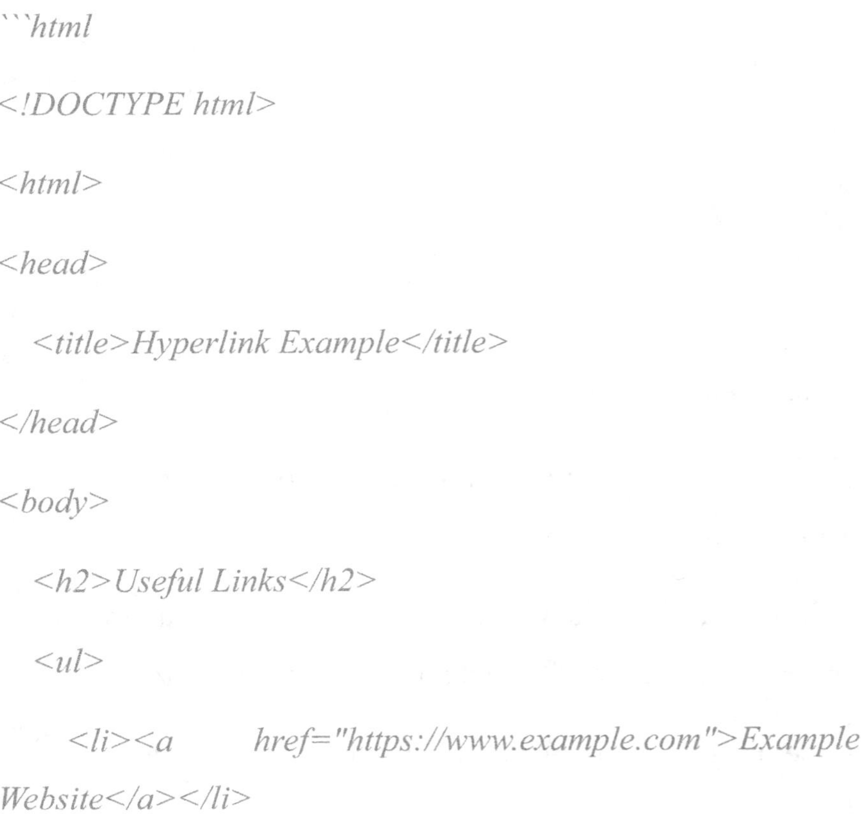

```html
<!DOCTYPE html>
<html>
<head>
  <title>Hyperlink Example</title>
</head>
<body>
  <h2>Useful Links</h2>
  <ul>
    <li><a href="https://www.example.com">Example Website</a></li>
```

```html
    <li><a href="page.html">Another Page</a></li>

    <li><a href="documents/document.pdf">Download PDF</a></li>

  </ul>


  <h2>Contact Us</h2>

  <p>If you have any questions, feel free to <a href="mailto:info@example.com">email us</a>.</p>

</body>

</html>

```

In the example above:

- The first list item creates a hyperlink to an external website using the full URL.

- The second list item creates a hyperlink to another page within the same website using a relative URL.

- The third list item creates a hyperlink to a PDF document in a subdirectory.

- The email link in the "Contact Us" section uses the `mailto:` protocol to open the user's default email client and populate the recipient's email address.

When creating hyperlinks, you can use either absolute URLs (complete web addresses) or relative URLs (paths relative to the current page's location) to link to different resources. Hyperlinks are essential for navigation and providing users with a seamless browsing experience.

LINKING TO EXTERNAL WEBSITES

Linking to external websites in HTML is a common practice for providing references or directing users to other online resources. You can use the `<a>` (anchor) element to create hyperlinks to external websites. Here's how you can do it:

```html

<!DOCTYPE html>

<html>

<head>
```

```html
    <title>External Website Links</title>

</head>

<body>

  <h2>Useful Websites</h2>

  <ul>

    <li><a href="https://www.example.com"
target="_blank">Example Website</a></li>

    <li><a href="https://www.openai.com"
target="_blank">OpenAI Official Site</a></li>

    <li><a href="https://www.wikipedia.org"
target="_blank">Wikipedia</a></li>

  </ul>

</body>

</html>

```

In the example above:

- The `href` attribute specifies the URL of the external website
you want to link to.

- The `target="_blank"` attribute opens the linked page in a new browser tab or window, allowing users to keep your website open while exploring the linked content.

When linking to external websites, it's generally a good practice to set `target="_blank"` for a better user experience. However, be mindful not to overuse this, as opening too many new tabs can become overwhelming for users.

LINKING WITHIN YOUR WEBSITE

Linking within your website using relative URLs is a fundamental aspect of web development. Relative URLs allow you to create links between different pages within your website. Here's how you can link to different pages within your own site:

Assume you have the following directory structure:

- *index.html*

- *about.html*

- *services.html*

- *contact.html*

```html
<!DOCTYPE html>
<html>
<head>
  <title>Internal Links</title>
</head>
<body>
  <nav>
    <ul>
      <li><a href="index.html">Home</a></li>
      <li><a href="about.html">About</a></li>
      <li><a href="services.html">Services</a></li>
      <li><a href="contact.html">Contact</a></li>
    </ul>
  </nav>
```

```html
<h1>Welcome to Our Website</h1>

<p>Explore our <a href="services.html">services</a> to learn more.</p>


<footer>

    <p>&copy; 2023 Your Website. All rights reserved.</p>

</footer>

</body>

</html>
```

In the example above:

- The `<a>` elements within the `<nav>` section create navigation links to other pages within the same directory.

- The link in the main content of the page uses a relative URL to link to the "services.html" page.

- The footer includes a copyright notice.

Using relative URLs makes your links flexible and adaptable, ensuring that your links continue to work even if you move or rename files or directories within your website.

ADDING IMAGES TO YOUR PAGE

To add images to your HTML page, you can use the `<img>` (image) element. Here's how you can do it:

Assume you have an image file named "example.jpg" in the same directory as your HTML file:

```html
<!DOCTYPE html>

<html>

<head>

    <title>Adding Images</title>

</head>

<body>

    <h1>Welcome to Our Website</h1>

    <p>Check out this image:</p>
```

```html
<img src="example.jpg" alt="An example image">

<p>Image source: <a href="example.jpg">example.jpg</a></p>

</body>

</html>
```

In the example above:

- The `<img>` element is used to display the image. The `src` attribute specifies the image file's relative URL.

- The `alt` attribute provides alternative text for the image. This text is displayed if the image can't be loaded or for accessibility purposes.

- The link below the image provides a direct link to the image file.

Remember to replace "example.jpg" with the actual filename and extension of your image. You can adjust the attributes and styles of the `<img>` element to customize how the image is displayed on your webpage.

IMAGE ATTRIBUTES

When adding images to your HTML page using the `<img>` element, you can use various attributes to control the appearance and behavior of the images. Here are some commonly used attributes:

- `src`: Specifies the source URL of the image.

- `alt`: Provides alternative text that is displayed when the image cannot be loaded, or for accessibility purposes.

- `width`: Sets the width of the image in pixels or as a percentage of its parent container.

- `height`: Sets the height of the image in pixels or as a percentage of its parent container.

- `title`: Adds a tooltip that appears when the user hovers over the image.

- `class`: Assigns a CSS class to the image for styling.

- `style`: Allows you to apply inline CSS styles to the image.

Here's an example of using some of these attributes:

```html
<!DOCTYPE html>

<html>

<head>

  <title>Image Attributes Example</title>

</head>

<body>

  <h1>Welcome to Our Website</h1>

  <img src="example.jpg" alt="An example image" width="300" height="200">

  <p>This is a beautiful <img src="flower.jpg" alt="Flower" title="Colorful Flower" class="rounded" style="border: 1px solid black;">.</p>

</body>

</html>
```

In the example above:

- The first image uses the `width` and `height` attributes to set specific dimensions for the image.

- The second image uses the `title` attribute to display a tooltip when hovering over the image. It also uses the `class` attribute to apply the "rounded" CSS class for styling, and the `style` attribute to add a black border.

You can combine these attributes to achieve the desired appearance and behavior for your images on the webpage.

CREATING FORMS

Creating forms in HTML allows you to collect user input, such as text, selections, and choices. Forms are often used for user registration, contact forms, surveys, and more. Here's how you can create a simple form:

```html
<!DOCTYPE html>

<html>

<head>

  <title>Creating Forms</title>

</head>

<body>

  <h2>Contact Us</h2>

    <form action="submit.php" method="post">

      <label for="name">Name:</label>

      <input type="text" id="name" name="name" required>
```

```html
    <label for="email">Email:</label>

    <input type="email" id="email" name="email"
required>


    <label for="message">Message:</label>

    <textarea id="message" name="message" rows="4"
required></textarea>


    <button type="submit">Submit</button>

  </form>

</body>

</html>
```

In the example above:

- The `<form>` element is used to create the form. The `action`
attribute specifies where the form data will be sent when the

user submits it. The `method` attribute defines how the data will be sent (GET or POST).

- `<label>` elements are associated with form controls for better accessibility.

- `<input>` elements create text fields. The `type` attribute defines the input type (text, email, etc.), and the `name` attribute provides a name for the input field.

- `<textarea>` creates a multi-line text area for longer input.

- The `required` attribute makes fields mandatory.

- The `<button>` element creates a submit button to send the form data.

In this example, the form data would be sent to a server-side script specified in the `action` attribute. You'll need to set up server-side code (like PHP or other server-side languages) to process the form data and take appropriate actions.

Creating forms in HTML allows you to collect user input, such as text, selections, and choices. Forms are often used for user registration, contact forms, surveys, and more. Here's how you can create a simple form:

```html
<!DOCTYPE html>
<html>
<head>
  <title>Creating Forms</title>
</head>
<body>
  <h2>Contact Us</h2>

  <form action="submit.php" method="post">
    <label for="name">Name:</label>
    <input type="text" id="name" name="name" required>

    <label for="email">Email:</label>
    <input type="email" id="email" name="email" required>
```

```
    <label for="message">Message:</label>

    <textarea id="message" name="message" rows="4"
required></textarea>


    <button type="submit">Submit</button>

  </form>

</body>

</html>

```
```

In the example above:

- The `<form>` element is used to create the form. The `action`
attribute specifies where the form data will be sent when the
user submits it. The `method` attribute defines how the data
will be sent (GET or POST).

- `<label>` elements are associated with form controls for
better accessibility.
```

- `<input>` elements create text fields. The `type` attribute defines the input type (text, email, etc.), and the `name` attribute provides a name for the input field.

- `<textarea>` creates a multi-line text area for longer input.

- The `required` attribute makes fields mandatory.

- The `<button>` element creates a submit button to send the form data.

In this example, the form data would be sent to a server-side script specified in the `action` attribute. You'll need to set up server-side code (like PHP or other server-side languages) to process the form data and take appropriate actions.

Here's an example of a simple contact form:

```html
<!DOCTYPE html>

<html>

<head>

    <title>Contact Form Example</title>

</head>
```

```html
<body>

  <h2>Contact Us</h2>

    <form action="submit.php" method="post">

    <label for="name">Name:</label>

    <input type="text" id="name" name="name"
required><br>


    <label for="email">Email:</label>

    <input type="email" id="email" name="email"
required><br>


    <label for="message">Message:</label><br>

    <textarea id="message" name="message" rows="4"
cols="50" required></textarea><br>


    <button type="submit">Submit</button>

  </form>

</body>
```

</html>

```
```

In this example:

- The `<form>` element is used to create the form. The `action` attribute specifies the URL where the form data will be sent when the user submits it. The `method` attribute defines how the data will be sent (POST or GET).

- `<label>` elements are associated with form controls for better accessibility.

- `<input>` elements create text fields. The `type` attribute defines the input type (text, email, etc.), and the `name` attribute provides a name for the input field. The `required` attribute makes the fields mandatory.

- `<textarea>` creates a multi-line text area for longer input. The `rows` and `cols` attributes specify the dimensions of the text area.

- The `<button>` element creates a submit button to send the form data.

Remember that this is just a basic example. In a real-world scenario, you would need to handle the form data on the server side using a programming language like PHP, Python, or JavaScript (Node.js) to process the data and take appropriate actions based on user input.

INPUT TYPES (TEXT, PASSWORD, RADIO. CHECKBOX, ETC)

Certainly! HTML provides various input types that you can use to collect different types of user input. Here's an overview of some commonly used input types:

1. Text Input (`type="text"`): Creates a single-line text input field.

```html
<input type="text" name="username" placeholder="Username">
```

2. Password Input (`type="password"`): Creates a password input field, where the entered text is masked for security.

```html
```

```html
<input type="password" name="password" placeholder="Password">
```

3. Radio Buttons (`type="radio"`): **Creates a set of radio buttons, allowing users to select one option from multiple choices.**

```html
<input type="radio" name="gender" value="male"> Male
<input type="radio" name="gender" value="female"> Female
```

4. Checkboxes (`type="checkbox"`): **Creates checkboxes that users can check or uncheck.**

```html
<input type="checkbox" name="subscribe" value="yes"> Subscribe to newsletter
<input type="checkbox" name="terms" value="agree" required> I agree to the terms and conditions
```

5. Number Input (`type="number"`): Creates an input field for numeric values.

```html
<input type="number" name="quantity" min="1" max="10" step="1">
```

6. Email Input (`type="email"`): Creates an input field for email addresses, with built-in validation.

```html
<input type="email" name="email" placeholder="Email">
```

7. Textarea (`<textarea>`): Creates a multi-line text input area.

```html
<textarea name="message" rows="4" cols="50" placeholder="Your message"></textarea>
```

8. File Input (`type="file"`): Creates a file upload input field.

```html
```

```
<input type="file" name="file">
```

9. Date Input (`type="date"`): Creates an input field for selecting a date.

```html
<input type="date" name="dob">
```

10. Submit Button (`type="submit"`): Creates a button to submit the form.

```html
<button type="submit">Submit</button>
```

These are just a few examples of the input types available in HTML. Each input type serves a specific purpose and can be used to collect various types of user input. You can combine these input types to create forms tailored to your specific needs.

FORM SUBMISSION

Form submission in HTML involves sending the user's input data to a server for further processing or storage. To achieve form submission, you need to define the `action` attribute in the `<form>` element, which specifies where the form data should be sent. You also need to define the `method` attribute to specify how the data should be sent (using the HTTP POST or GET method).

Here's an example of a basic form with form submission:

```html
<!DOCTYPE html>
<html>
<head>
  <title>Form Submission Example</title>
</head>
<body>
  <h2>Contact Us</h2>
```

```html
<form action="process.php" method="post">

    <label for="name">Name:</label>

    <input type="text" id="name" name="name"
required><br>


    <label for="email">Email:</label>

    <input type="email" id="email" name="email"
required><br>


    <label for="message">Message:</label><br>

    <textarea id="message" name="message" rows="4"
cols="50" required></textarea><br>


    <button type="submit">Submit</button>

  </form>

</body>

</html>

```

In this example:

- The `action` attribute in the `<form>` element specifies the URL (`process.php`) to which the form data will be submitted.

- The `method` attribute is set to "post," indicating that the form data will be sent via the HTTP POST method.

- The input fields (`<input>`, `<textarea>`) have `name` attributes that will be used to identify the form data on the server.

- The submit button triggers the form submission when clicked.

On the server side (e.g., in a PHP script), you would use the `$_POST` or `$_GET` superglobal arrays to access the form data submitted by the user. Here's a simple example of how you might process the form data in a PHP script named "process.php":

```php
<?php

if ($_SERVER["REQUEST_METHOD"] == "POST") {

    $name = $_POST["name"];
```

```php
$email = $_POST["email"];

$message = $_POST["message"];

    // Process and store the data as needed

    // Redirect user after form submission

header("Location: thank_you.html");

exit;

}

?>

```

Remember that form submission is just the beginning. Depending on your requirements, you might want to add validation, sanitization, database interactions, and more to handle the submitted data effectively.

USING SEMANTIC TAGS (HEADER, NAV, MAIN, ARTICLE, SECTION, FOOTER)

Semantic HTML elements provide more meaning and structure to your web page content. They help improve accessibility, search engine optimization, and overall readability of your code. Here's how you can use some common semantic elements in your HTML:

1. `<header>`: Represents the header of a section or a page.

```html
<header>
  <h1>Welcome to My Website</h1>
  <nav>
    <ul>
      <li><a href="#">Home</a></li>
      <li><a href="#">About</a></li>
      <li><a href="#">Services</a></li>
      <li><a href="#">Contact</a></li>
```

```
    </ul>

  </nav>

</header>
```

2. `<nav>`: Represents navigation links.

```html
<nav>

  <ul>

    <li><a href="#">Home</a></li>

    <li><a href="#">Products</a></li>

    <li><a href="#">Blog</a></li>

    <li><a href="#">Contact</a></li>

  </ul>

</nav>

```

3. `<main>`: Represents the main content of the document.

```html
```

```html
<main>

  <article>

    <h2>Article Title</h2>

    <p>This is the content of the article.</p>

  </article>

  <section>

    <h2>Featured Products</h2>

    <ul>

      <li>Product 1</li>

      <li>Product 2</li>

      <li>Product 3</li>

    </ul>

  </section>

</main>

```

4. `<article>`: Represents a self-contained composition that can be distributed independently from the rest of the content.

```html
<article>

    <h2>Article Title</h2>

    <p>This is the content of the article.</p>

    <footer>

        <p>Published on August 6, 2023</p>

    </footer>

</article>
```

5. `<section>`: Represents a thematic grouping of content.

```html
<section>

    <h2>Our Services</h2>

    <ul>

        <li>Service 1</li>

        <li>Service 2</li>

        <li>Service 3</li>
```

```
    </ul>

</section>

```

6. `<footer>`: Represents the footer of a section or a page.

```html

<footer>

  <p>&copy; 2023 Your Company. All rights reserved.</p>

</footer>

```

Using these semantic elements not only improves the structure of your HTML but also helps search engines and screen readers understand the content and hierarchy of your page better. It's a best practice to use semantic elements whenever possible to create a more accessible and meaningful web experience.

IMPROVING ACCESSIBILITY

Improving accessibility is crucial to ensure that your website can be used by a wide range of people, including those with disabilities. Here are some ways you can enhance the accessibility of your web content:

1. Use Semantic HTML: As discussed earlier, using semantic HTML elements like `<header>`, `<nav>`, `<main>`, `<article>`, `<section>`, and `<footer>` provides a clear structure to your content, making it easier for screen readers and search engines to understand.

2. Provide Alternative Text for Images: Use the `alt` attribute to provide meaningful descriptions for images. This helps users with visual impairments understand the content of the images.

3. Create Keyboard-Friendly Designs: Ensure that all interactive elements, such as links and form fields, can be easily navigated using a keyboard. This is essential for users who can't use a mouse.

4. Use ARIA Roles and Attributes: ARIA (Accessible Rich Internet Applications) roles and attributes can enhance the accessibility of complex web applications. For example, you can use `role="button"` to indicate interactive elements that behave like buttons.

5. *Test with Screen Readers:* Regularly test your website with screen readers to understand how users with visual

impairments experience your content. This can help you identify accessibility issues and address them.

6. Provide Sufficient Color Contrast: Ensure that text has sufficient contrast against its background to make it readable for all users, including those with low vision.

7. Use Responsive Design: Create a responsive design that adapts to different screen sizes, making your content accessible on various devices, including mobile phones and tablets.

8. Provide Captions for Videos: If you have videos on your website, provide closed captions or subtitles to make the content accessible to users who are deaf or hard of hearing.

9. Avoid Using Only Color to Convey Information: Information should not solely rely on color. Use other cues like text or icons to convey important information.

10. Use Focus Indicators: Make sure that focus indicators are clearly visible when navigating through your website using a keyboard. This helps users understand where they are on the page.

11. Offer Resize Options: Allow users to adjust text size without breaking the layout of your website. This is important for users who need larger text.

12. Provide Descriptive Links: **Make** link text descriptive so users understand where the link will take them. Avoid using generic terms like "click here."

13. Test with Web Accessibility Tools: **Utilize** web accessibility evaluation tools to identify potential issues and get suggestions for improving accessibility.

By implementing these practices, you can create a more inclusive web experience for all users and ensure that your content is accessible to everyone, regardless of their abilities.

INTRODUCTION TO CASCADING STYLE SHEET

Cascading Style Sheets, commonly referred to as CSS, is a language used to control the presentation and styling of HTML documents. It allows you to define how your web content should be displayed, including aspects like layout, colors, fonts, spacing, and more. CSS separates the content of your web page from its visual design, making it easier to maintain and apply consistent styles across your website.

Here's a brief introduction to CSS:

1. Selectors: CSS uses selectors to target HTML elements you want to style. Selectors can be based on element names, classes, IDs, attributes, and more.

2. Properties and Values: CSS rules consist of properties and values. Properties define what aspect of an element you want to style (e.g., `color`, `font-size`, `margin`). Values specify how you want that aspect to appear (e.g., `red`, `16px`, `20px 10px`).

3. Declaration Block: A declaration block contains one or more property-value pairs enclosed in curly braces `{}`. Multiple declarations are separated by semicolons.

4. CSS Rule: A CSS rule consists of a selector followed by a declaration block. It defines which elements the styles should be applied to and what styles should be applied.

Example of a simple CSS rule:

```css
h1 {
    color: blue;
    font-size: 24px;
}
```

5. Internal CSS: You can include CSS directly within your HTML file using the `<style>` tag within the `<head>` section.

```html
<head>
  <style>
    h1 {
      color: blue;
      font-size: 24px;
    }
  </style>
</head>
```

6. *External CSS:* It's a common practice to link an external CSS file to your HTML file using the `<link>` tag. This keeps your HTML and CSS separate, making it easier to manage and update styles.

```html
<head>
  <link rel="stylesheet" href="styles.css">
</head>
```

7. *CSS Selectors:* CSS provides a variety of selectors, including:

- *Element selector (`element`)*

- *Class selector (`.classname`)*

- *ID selector (`#idname`)*

- *Descendant selector (`parent child`)*

- *Pseudo-class selector (`:hover`, `:active`)*

- *Attribute selector (`[attribute=value]`)*

CSS is a powerful tool that allows you to transform the appearance of your web content, providing a visually pleasing and consistent user experience across different devices and screen sizes. It's essential for creating modern and appealing websites.

STYLING TEXT AND BACKGROUNDS

Styling text and backgrounds using CSS allows you to enhance the visual appeal and readability of your web page. You can change fonts, colors, spacing, and more. Here's how you can style text and backgrounds using CSS:

1. Changing Text Color (`color` Property):

You can change the color of text using the `color` property.

```css
p {
    color: blue;
}
```

2. Changing Font (`font-family` Property):

You can specify different font families for your text using the `font-family` property.

```css
body {

    font-family: Arial, sans-serif;

}
```

3. *Changing Font Size (`font-size` Property):*

You can adjust the size of your text using the `font-size` property.

```css
h1 {
  font-size: 32px;
}
```

4. *Styling Text Weight (`font-weight` Property):*

You can control the weight (boldness) of text using the `font-weight` property.

```css
strong {
  font-weight: bold;
}
```

You can change the background color of elements using the `background-color` property.

```css
section {
    background-color: #f0f0f0;
}
```

6. *Adding Padding (`padding` Property):*

You can add spacing between the content and the edges of an element using the `padding` property.

```css
div {
    padding: 10px;
}
```

7. Adding Margins (`margin` Property):

You can control the spacing between elements using the `margin` property.

```css
p {
    margin-bottom: 20px;
}
```

8. Text Alignment (`text-align` Property):

You can align text within an element using the `text-align` property.

```css
h1 {
    text-align: center;
}
```

9. Changing Text Decoration (`text-decoration` Property):

You can apply decorations like underlines or strikethroughs to text using the `text-decoration` property.

```css
a {
    text-decoration: none;
}
u {
    text-decoration: underline;
}
```

These are just a few examples of how you can style text and backgrounds using CSS. You can combine these properties to achieve various visual effects and create a unique design for your web page. Remember to test your styles on different devices and screen sizes to ensure a consistent and pleasant user experience.

ADDING BORDERS AND MARGINS

Certainly! You can use CSS to add borders and margins to elements on your web page. Here's how you can do it:

1. Adding Borders (`border` Property):

You can use the `border` property to add borders to elements. It can include properties for border width, style, and color.

```css
/ Adding a border to an element /
div {
    border: 1px solid #000;
}
```

2. Changing Border Style (`border-style` Property):

You can change the style of the border using the `border-style` property. Common values include `solid`, `dashed`, `dotted`, and `none`.

```css
/ Changing the border style /

p {

    border: 2px dashed red;

}
```

3. Changing Border Color (`border-color` Property):

You can change the color of the border using the `border-color` property.

```css
/ Changing the border color /

a {

    border: 1px solid blue;

    border-color: blue;

}
```

4. Changing Border Width (`border-width` Property):

You can change the width of the border using the `border-width` property.

```css
/ Changing the border width /
button {
    border: 3px solid green;
    border-width: 3px;
}
```

5. Adding Margins (`margin` Property):

You can use the `margin` property to add spacing around an element. It can include values for top, right, bottom, and left margins.

```css
/ Adding margins to an element /
```

```
h2 {

    margin: 20px;

}
```

6. *Using Margin Shorthand:*

You can also use the shorthand `margin` property to define margins for all sides or individual sides.

```css

/ Using margin shorthand /

p {

    margin: 10px 20px; / top and bottom margins are 10px, left and right margins are 20px /

}

```

```css

/ Specifying margins for individual sides /

div {

    margin-top: 10px;
```

```
    margin-right: 20px;

    margin-bottom: 30px;

    margin-left: 40px;

}
```

Adding borders and margins using CSS can help create separation between elements and enhance the visual appearance of your web page. Remember to balance the use of these properties to ensure a clean and organized design.

CREATING TABLES

Creating tables in HTML allows you to organize and display tabular data. Tables are composed of rows (`<tr>`) and columns (`<td>` for table data cells or `<th>` for table header cells). *Here's how you can create a basic table:*

```html
<!DOCTYPE html>

<html>

<head>

  <title>Creating Tables</title>

</head>

<body>

  <h2>Student Grades</h2>

  <table border="1">

    <tr>

      <th>Student ID</th>

      <th>Name</th>
```

```html
    <th>Math</th>

    <th>Science</th>

    <th>English</th>

  </tr>

  <tr>

    <td>101</td>

    <td>John Doe</td>

    <td>90</td>

    <td>85</td>

    <td>92</td>

  </tr>

  <tr>

    <td>102</td>

    <td>Jane Smith</td>

    <td>88</td>

    <td>92</td>

    <td>89</td>
```

```
    </tr>

  </table>

</body>

</html>
```

In this example:

- The `<table>` element creates the table container.

- `<tr>` elements define table rows.

- `<th>` elements define table header cells, which are typically used for column headers.

- `<td>` elements define table data cells, which contain the actual data.

- The `border="1"` attribute adds a border around the table for better visibility.

You can further style your table using CSS to adjust borders, colors, spacing, and more. Additionally, you can use the `colspan` and `rowspan` attributes to span columns or rows if needed.

Tables are useful for displaying structured data, but be cautious when using them for layout purposes. For modern web layout, it's recommended to use CSS for positioning and styling instead of relying solely on tables.

ADDING ROWS AND COLUMNS

To add rows and columns to a table in HTML, you can use the `<tr>` (table row) element for rows and the `<td>` (table data cell) element for columns. Here's how you can add rows and columns to an existing table:

```html
<!DOCTYPE html>

<html>

<head>

    <title>Adding Rows and Columns</title>

</head>

<body>

    <h2>Student Grades</h2>
```

```
<table border="1">

  <tr>

    <th>Student ID</th>

    <th>Name</th>

    <th>Math</th>

    <th>Science</th>

    <th>English</th>

  </tr>

  <tr>

    <td>101</td>

    <td>John Doe</td>

    <td>90</td>

    <td>85</td>

    <td>92</td>

  </tr>

  <tr>

    <td>102</td>
```

```html
      <td>Jane Smith</td>

      <td>88</td>

      <td>92</td>

      <td>89</td>

  </tr>

  <!-- Adding a new row -->

  <tr>

      <td>103</td>

      <td>Alice Johnson</td>

      <td>95</td>

      <td>78</td>

      <td>91</td>

  </tr>

  </table>

</body>

</html>
```

In the example above, a new row has been added using the `<tr>` element. Within each row, you can use `<td>` elements to define the cells (columns) of the table. The new row with student information has been added after the existing rows.

To add additional columns, simply add more `<td>` elements within each `<tr>` element. Make sure each row has the same number of cells as the header row (if you want to maintain the column structure).

You can also use the `colspan` and `rowspan` attributes to span columns or rows when you need to merge cells for special purposes.

TABLE HEADERS AND DATAS

In HTML, you can use the `<th>` element for table headers (usually placed in the first row) and the `<td>` element for table data cells. This helps define the purpose of each cell in the table and improves the semantic structure of your tabular data. Here's how you can use table headers and data cells:

```html
<!DOCTYPE html>
<html>
<head>
  <title>Table Headers and Data</title>
</head>
<body>
  <h2>Monthly Expenses</h2>
  <table border="1">
    <tr>
      <th>Month</th>
      <th>Utilities</th>
      <th>Food</th>
      <th>Transportation</th>
      <th>Total</th>
    </tr>
    <tr>
```

```html
        <td>January</td>

        <td>$150</td>

        <td>$200</td>

        <td>$100</td>

        <td>$450</td>

    </tr>

    <tr>

        <td>February</td>

        <td>$140</td>

        <td>$180</td>

        <td>$110</td>

        <td>$430</td>

    </tr>

  </table>

</body>

</html>
```

In this example:

- The first row uses `<th>` elements to define table headers. These headers describe the content of the columns.

- The subsequent rows use `<td>` elements to define the table data cells. Each cell contains specific data related to the corresponding header.

Using `<th>` elements for headers provides better semantic meaning and accessibility for screen readers, which can distinguish between header cells and data cells. This is especially useful for data tables with complex structures.

When creating data tables, ensure that the headers and data cells are aligned correctly. Additionally, you can use CSS to style the table headers differently from the data cells, such as by applying a different background color or font style.

AUDIO AND VIDEO ELEMENT

The `<audio>` and `<video>` elements in HTML allow you to embed audio and video content directly into your web pages. Here's how you can use these elements:

1. Embedding Audio (`<audio>`):

You can use the `<audio>` element to embed audio content. Provide a source URL using the `src` attribute, and optionally include controls for playback and volume control.

```html
<audio controls>
  <source src="music.mp3" type="audio/mpeg">
  Your browser does not support the audio element.
</audio>
```

In the example above, the browser will try to play the "music.mp3" audio file. If the browser doesn't support the audio element or the specified audio format, the fallback text "Your browser does not support the audio element." Will be displayed.

2. Embedding Video (`<video>`):

You can use the `<video>` element to embed video content. Similar to the `<audio>` element, provide a source URL using the `src` attribute and include controls for playback.

```html
<video controls width="480" height="270">
  <source src="video.mp4" type="video/mp4">
  Your browser does not support the video element.
</video>
```

In this example, the browser will try to play the "video.mp4" video file. You can also specify the `width` and `height` attributes to set the dimensions of the video player.

Both `<audio>` and `<video>` elements support various attributes for controlling playback, appearance, and more. You can customize these attributes to suit your needs. Additionally, consider providing multiple source URLs in different formats to ensure compatibility with various browsers and devices.

Remember that different browsers support different audio and video formats, so it's a good practice to include multiple source types to ensure your content works across different platforms.

CANVAS FOR GRAPHICS

The HTML `<canvas>` element is a powerful feature that allows you to create and manipulate graphics directly within your web page using JavaScript. It provides a drawing surface on which you can create various visual elements, animations, games, and interactive experiences. Here's how you can use the `<canvas>` element for graphics:

```html
<!DOCTYPE html>

<html>

<head>

  <title>Canvas Graphics</title>

</head>

<body>

  <h2>Canvas Example</h2>

  <canvas id="myCanvas" width="400" height="200"></canvas>

  <script>

    // Get the canvas element

    var canvas = document.getElementById("myCanvas");


    // Get the drawing context (2D)
```

```html
    var ctx = canvas.getContext("2d");

    // Draw a rectangle
    ctx.fillStyle = "blue";
    ctx.fillRect(50, 50, 100, 100);

    // Draw a circle
    ctx.beginPath();
    ctx.arc(250, 100, 50, 0, 2  Math.PI);
    ctx.fillStyle = "green";
    ctx.fill();
    ctx.closePath();
  </script>
</body>
</html>
```

n this example:

- The `<canvas>` element is used to create a drawing surface with a specified width and height.

- The `<script>` section contains JavaScript code that interacts with the canvas.

- The `getContext("2d")` method gets a 2D drawing context, which provides methods for drawing shapes, lines, text, and more.

- `fillRect()` is used to draw a filled rectangle with a specified position and size.

- `beginPath()` starts a new path for drawing.

- `arc()` draws a circular arc with specified center, radius, start angle, and end angle.

- `fill()` fills the current path w7PMES```html

```html
<!DOCTYPE html>

<html>

<head>

    <title>Geolocation Example</title>
```

```html
</head>

<body>

  <h2>Geolocation Example</h2>

  <p id="location"></p>


  <script>

    if ("geolocation" in navigator) {


navigator.geolocation.getCurrentPosition(function(position) {

        var latitude = position.coords.latitude;

        var longitude = position.coords.longitude;


document.getElementById("location").textContent        =
"Latitude: " + latitude + ", Longitude: " + longitude;

      });

    } else {
```

```
      document.getElementById("location").textContent =
"Geolocation is not supported by this browser.";

    }

  </script>

</body>

</html>

```

In this example, the Geolocation API is used to retrieve the user's latitude and longitude. If the browser supports geolocation, the coordinates are displayed; otherwise, a message indicating lack of support is shown.

Embedding Maps using Google Maps API:
To embed interactive maps into your web pages, you can use the Google Maps JavaScript API. You need to sign up for an API key from the Google Cloud Platform to use this service.

```html
<!DOCTYPE html>
<html>
<head>
  <title>Google Maps Example</title>
  <script
src="https://maps.googleapis.com/maps/api/js?key=YOUR_API_KEY&callback=initMap" async
defer></script>
</head>
<body>
  <h2>Google Maps Example</h2>
  <div id="map" style="width: 100%; height: 400px;"></div>
```

```html
<script>

    function initMap() {

        var location = { lat: 37.7749, lng: -122.4194 }; // San Francisco coordinates

        var map = new google.maps.Map(document.getElementById("map"), {

            center: location,

            zoom: 10

        });

        var marker = new google.maps.Marker({

            position: location,

            map: map,

            title: "San Francisco"

        }); }

    </script>

</body>

</html>
```

Replace `YOUR_API_KEY` with the actual API key you obtained from the Google Cloud Platform. This example initializes a map centered on San Francisco and places a marker on that location.

Both geolocation and maps are powerful tools for enhancing user experience and providing location-based features on your website. Keep in mind that geolocation requires user permission, and you should always ensure user privacy and security when using these features.

USING HTML VALIDATORS

HTML validators are tools that help you ensure that your HTML code is well-formed, adheres to HTML standards, and follows best practices. Validating your HTML code helps improve the quality of your website, ensures cross-browser compatibility, and contributes to better search engine optimization. Here are some popular HTML validators you can use:

1. W3C Markup Validation Service:

The World Wide Web Consortium (W3C) offers a free Markup Validation Service that checks your HTML code against W3C standards. It highlights errors, warnings, and suggestions for improvement.

You can access the service at: https://validator.w3.org/

2. Nu HTML Checker (Validator.nu):

Nu HTML Checker is another validator that helps you validate HTML5 and provides detailed reports on issues in your code. It's maintained by the HTML Working Group.

Access the validator at: https://validator.nu/

3. W3C CSS Validation Service:

While not directly an HTML validator, the W3C CSS Validation Service is useful for validating your CSS stylesheets. Proper CSS is essential for the correct presentation of your HTML content.

You can access the CSS validator at: *https://jigsaw.w3.org/css-validator/*

4. Browser Developer Tools:

Modern web browsers come with built-in developer tools that often include HTML validation. These tools highlight syntax errors and give you real-time feedback as you develop.

For example, in Google Chrome, you can right-click on a web page, select "Inspect," and navigate to the "Console" tab to see HTML validation messages.

Using these validators, you can input the URL of your web page or paste your HTML code directly into the validator interface. The tools will then analyze your code and provide a detailed report with information about any issues found.

Remember that while validation is important, not all warnings are critical, and some can be ignored based on your specific requirements. The main goal is to ensure that your code is well-structured and adheres to the standards to create a better user experience and maintainability.

COMMON HTML ERRORS AND HOW TO FIX THEM

Here are some common HTML errors and how to fix them:

1. Unclosed Tags:

Unclosed tags occur when you forget to close an HTML tag. For example:

```html

<p>This is an unclosed paragraph.

<div>Another unclosed tag.

```

To fix this, ensure that all opening tags have corresponding closing tags:

```html

<p>This is a closed paragraph.</p>

<div>Another closed tag.</div>

```

2. Mismatched Tags:

Mismatched tags occur when you mix up opening and closing tags. For example:

```html
<b>This is <i>incorrect</b></i>
```

To fix this, ensure that opening and closing tags match and nest properly:

```html
<b>This is <i>correct</i></b>
```

3. Missing Quotes in Attributes:

Missing quotes in attributes can lead to parsing errors. For example:

```html
<a href=https://www.example.com>Incorrect link</a>
```

To fix this, use double or single quotes around attribute values:

```html
<a href="https://www.example.com">Correct link</a>
```

4. Using Deprecated Elements:

Using deprecated elements like `<center>` or `<font>` can result in rendering issues in modern browsers. Instead, use CSS for styling and alignment.

5. Non-Self-Closing Tags:

Some tags, like `<img>` or `<input>`, are self-closing and don't require a closing tag. Forgetting this can cause errors.

```html
<img src="image.jpg"></img> <!-- Incorrect -->

<input type="text" value="Example"> <!-- Incorrect -->
```

To fix this, remove the unnecessary closing tags:

```html

<img src="image.jpg"> <!-- Correct -->

<input type="text" value="Example"> <!-- Correct -->

```


6. Missing Doctype Declaration:

A missing or incorrect doctype declaration can cause compatibility and rendering issues. Always include a doctype declaration at the beginning of your HTML document.

```html

<!DOCTYPE html>

<html>

<!-- Your HTML code here -->

</html>

```

7. Incorrect Nesting:

Incorrectly nesting elements can lead to unexpected results. For instance:

```html
<ul>
    <li>List item 1
    <li>List item 2</ul>
</ul>
```

To fix this, ensure proper nesting:

```html
<ul>
    <li>List item 1</li>
    <li>List item 2</li>
</ul>
```

8. Using Reserved Characters:

Certain characters like `<`, `>`, and `&` have special meanings in HTML. Use HTML entities to display them correctly.

```html
<p>5 > 3 is true</p> <!-- Incorrect -->

<p>5 &gt; 3 is true</p> <!-- Correct -->
```

9. Case Sensitivity:

HTML is case-insensitive, but it's recommended to use lowercase tags and attribute names for consistency and to avoid issues.

Correct: `<img src="image.jpg" alt="Description">`

Incorrect: `<IMG SRC="image.jpg" ALT="Description">`

10. Ignoring Quotes Around Attributes:

Although some browsers might tolerate it, it's best practice to include quotes around attribute values.

```html

<a href=https://www.example.com>Link</a>

<!-- Incorrect -->

<a href="https://www.example.com">Link</a>

<!-- Correct -->

```

Regularly validating your HTML using online validators or browser developer tools can help catch and fix these errors, ensuring that your web pages function correctly and consistently across different platforms.

CHOOSING A WEB HOSTING PROVIDER

Choosing a web hosting provider is an important decision that can impact the performance, security, and overall success of your website. Here are some key factors to consider when selecting a web hosting provider:

1. Type of Hosting:

   - Shared Hosting: Affordable and suitable for small websites. Your website shares server resources with other sites.

   - VPS Hosting: Offers more resources and control compared to shared hosting. You have your own virtual server.

   - Dedicated Hosting: Provides an entire physical server for your website. Offers maximum control and performance.

   - Cloud Hosting: Scalable and flexible hosting, where your site's resources can be adjusted based on demand.

2. Performance and Speed:

- Look for hosting providers that offer solid-state drives (SSDs) for faster data access.

- Check if they provide content delivery network (CDN) integration to improve loading times across different locations.

3. Uptime and Reliability:

- Choose a provider with a high uptime guarantee (99.9% or higher).

- Read reviews or seek recommendations to gauge the reliability of the hosting company.

4. Scalability:

- Consider future growth. Choose a provider that allows you to easily upgrade or downgrade your hosting plan.

5. Security Features:

- Look for providers that offer features like SSL certificates, regular backups, and firewall protection.

6. Support and Customer Service:

- 24/7 customer support can be crucial if you encounter issues with your website.

- Check if they offer multiple support channels like live chat, phone, and email.

7. Control Panel and User Interface:

- A user-friendly control panel makes it easier to manage your website, domains, and settings.

8. Price and Value:

- Compare pricing and features among different providers. Be cautious of extremely cheap hosting with limited resources.

- Consider the features included in the plan, such as the number of domains, storage, bandwidth, and email accounts.

9. Ease of Use and One-Click Installs:

- Many hosting providers offer one-click installations for popular content management systems (CMS) like WordPress.

10. Server Location:

- Choose a provider with server locations that are geographically close to your target audience for faster load times.

11. Backup and Restore Options:

- Regular backups are essential. Check if the provider offers automatic backups and easy restoration.

12. Terms of Service and Restrictions:

- Read the terms of service carefully to understand any limitations, resource usage, or restrictions.

13. Reviews and Reputation:

   - Research customer reviews and ratings to get an idea of the provider's reputation.

14. Migration Assistance:

   - If you're transferring an existing website, inquire about the provider's migration support.

15. Additional Services:

   - Some providers offer domain registration, website builder tools, and other extras.

Take your time to evaluate your options, and consider your website's specific needs and goals. It's a good idea to start with a hosting plan that meets your current requirements and allows room for growth as your website expands.

To upload your HTML files to a web hosting provider, you typically have a few options depending on the hosting environment and tools provided by your chosen provider. Here's a general step-by-step guide:

1. Choose a Web Hosting Provider:

If you haven't already, select a web hosting provider that suits your needs and offers the hosting type you require (shared, VPS, dedicated, etc.).

2. Get Your Hosting Account Details:

After signing up for a hosting plan, you'll receive account details that include login credentials and information about your server or hosting space.

3. Access Your Hosting Control Panel:

Most hosting providers offer a control panel (such as cPanel, Plesk, or a custom interface) where you can manage your hosting settings and upload files.

4. Locate the File Manager:

Within your hosting control panel, find the "File Manager" or a similar option. This is where you can upload and manage your website files.

5. Upload HTML Files:

In the File Manager, navigate to the directory where you want to upload your HTML files. This could be the root directory (often named `public_html` or `www`), or a subdirectory for a specific part of your website.

6. Upload Files Using the File Manager:

Use the File Manager's interface to upload your HTML files. This usually involves clicking an "Upload" button, selecting the files from your computer, and confirming the upload.

7. Set File Permissions (If Necessary):

Depending on the hosting environment, you might need to adjust file permissions to ensure proper access. Consult your hosting provider's documentation for guidance on setting file permissions.

8. Access Your Website:

Once your files are uploaded, you can access your website by entering your domain name in a web browser. The homepage (usually named `index.html`) should load automatically.

9. Test Your Website:

Browse through your website to ensure that all the elements are displaying correctly and that links are working.

10. Domain Configuration (If Needed):

If you've registered your domain with a separate provider, you might need to update your domain's DNS settings to point to your hosting provider's servers. Check your hosting provider's documentation for specific instructions.

11. Troubleshooting and Support:

If you encounter any issues during the upload process or while accessing your website, refer to your hosting provider's support resources or contact their customer support for assistance.

Remember that the process might vary slightly depending on your hosting provider, so it's a good idea to refer to their specific documentation or contact their support if you need further guidance.

To make your website live and accessible to visitors on the internet, you need to complete a few steps after uploading your HTML files to your web hosting provider. Here's what you need to do to make your site live:

1. Domain Configuration:

If you have a domain name registered with a separate domain registrar, you need to point it to your web hosting provider's servers. This is done by updating the domain's DNS (Domain Name System) settings to include the hosting provider's nameservers.

2. Update Nameservers:

Log in to your domain registrar's control panel and locate the DNS or Nameserver settings. Replace the default nameservers with the nameservers provided by your hosting provider. This step connects your domain to your hosting space.

3. DNS Propagation:

Keep in mind that DNS changes take time to propagate across the internet. This process can take a few hours to up to 48 hours. During this period, your website might not be accessible to everyone.

4. Verify Domain Connection:

Once DNS propagation is complete, you should be able to access your website by typing your domain name in a web browser. Make sure all your pages, images, and links work as expected.

5. Testing on Different Devices:

Test your website on different devices (desktop, tablet, smartphone) and different browsers to ensure it displays correctly and functions properly across various platforms.

6. Check for Broken Links:

Carefully check all links on your website to ensure they lead to the correct pages. Fix any broken or incorrect links.

7. SSL Certificate (If Applicable):

If your hosting plan includes an SSL certificate (for secure connections), make sure it's properly set up. Secure websites start with "https://" instead of "http://".

8. Search Engine Optimization (SEO):

If you want your website to be discoverable by search engines, make sure you optimize your pages with relevant keywords, meta descriptions, and other SEO techniques.

9. Google Analytics (Optional):

Consider adding Google Analytics tracking code to your website to gather insights about your visitors' behavior and engagement.

10. Backup Your Site:

Regularly backup your website's files and databases to ensure that you can restore your site if anything goes wrong.

11. Promote Your Site:

Once your site is live, share it with your audience through social media, email, and other marketing channels.

12. Regular Maintenance:

Continuously update and maintain your website to ensure it remains functional, secure, and up to date.

Remember that making your site live is just the beginning. Regularly update your content, monitor your site's performance, and respond to user feedback to provide the best experience for your visitors.

FURTHER LEARNING RESOURCES

There are some further learning resources to help you expand your knowledge of web development and related topics:

1. Online Learning Platforms:

    - [Codecademy](https://www.codecademy.com/)

    - [Coursera](https://www.coursera.org/)

    - [Udemy](https://www.udemy.com/)

    - [edX](https://www.edx.org/)

2. FreeCodeCamp:

A comprehensive platform that offers interactive coding challenges and projects covering HTML, CSS, JavaScript, and more:

[FreeCodeCamp](https://www.freecodecamp.org/)

3. MDN Web Docs:

A reputable resource by Mozilla for web development documentation and tutorials: [MDN Web Docs](https://developer.mozilla.org/)

4. W3Schools:

Provides tutorials, references, and interactive coding examples for HTML, CSS, JavaScript, and more: [W3Schools](https://www.w3schools.com/)

5. CSS-Tricks:

Offers articles, guides, and tutorials on CSS and front-end development: [CSS-Tricks](https://css-tricks.com/)

6. GitHub Learning Lab:

GitHub's interactive learning platform with practical exercises and projects: [GitHub Learning Lab] (https://lab.github.com/)

7. YouTube Channels:

   - [Traversy Media]
(https://www.youtube.com/user/TechGuyWeb)

   - [The Net Ninja]
(https://www.youtube.com/c/TheNetNinja)

   - [Academind]
(https://www.youtube.com/c/Academind)

   - [Kevin
Powell](https://www.youtube.com/user/KepowOb)

8. Books:

   - "HTML and CSS: Design and Build Websites" by Jon
Duckett

   - "JavaScript: The Good Parts" by Douglas Crockford

   - "Eloquent JavaScript" by Marijn Haverbeke

9. Coding Challenges and Practice:

- [LeetCode](https://leetcode.com/)

- [HackerRank]
(https://www.hackerrank.com/domains/tutorials/10-days-
of-javascript)

10. Web Development Blogs:

Follow blogs from experts in the field for the latest trends, tips, and best practices.

Remember that web development is a continuously evolving field, so it's important to keep learning and practicing regularly. Don't hesitate to explore different resources to find the ones that resonate with your learning style. As you gain experience, consider working on personal projects to apply what you've learned and build a portfolio of your work.

Here are some advanced HTML topics that you can explore to enhance your web development skills:

1. HTML Semantics:

Dive deeper into using semantic HTML elements like `<header>`, `<nav>`, `<main>`, `<article>`, `<section>`, and `<footer>` to improve the structure and accessibility of your web pages.

2. HTML Forms and Inputs:

Learn about advanced form features like input validation, custom form controls, HTML5 input types (such as date, email, number), and attributes like `pattern`, `min`, and `max`.

3. HTML Media Elements:

Explore more about embedding multimedia content using `<audio>`, `<video>`, and `<canvas>`, along with advanced attributes and customization options.

4. HTML Web Storage:

Understand how to use `localStorage` and `sessionStorage` to store data on the client side for improved user experiences and temporary data storage.

5. HTML Custom Data Attributes:

Learn about the `data-` attribute that allows you to store custom data directly in your HTML elements, useful for JavaScript interactions.

6. HTML Templates and Shadow DOM:

Discover HTML templates for reusable content and the Shadow DOM for creating encapsulated components.

7. HTML Meta Tags:

Explore advanced usage of meta tags for better SEO, social sharing, and optimization of web content.

8. HTML Accessibility:

Deepen your knowledge of web accessibility by understanding ARIA roles and attributes, and how to make your web content more usable for people with disabilities.

9. HTML Imports and Modules:

Explore the concept of HTML imports (importing HTML documents into other HTML documents) and the use of modern JavaScript modules.

10. Responsive Web Design:

Learn advanced techniques for creating responsive layouts, such as media queries, flexible grids, and fluid images, to ensure your site looks great on various devices.

11. HTML Preprocessors:

Explore tools like Pug (formerly Jade) and Haml that allow you to write more concise HTML using indentation-based syntax.

12. Web Components:

Dive into the world of web components, which are a set of technologies that enable you to create reusable custom elements with encapsulated functionality.

Remember that advanced topics often require a solid understanding of the foundational concepts. As you explore these areas, practice by building real-world projects to apply your knowledge and gain hands-on experience. Experimenting with different techniques and incorporating them into your projects will help you become a more well-rounded web developer.

9 798858 389576